From

First Aid For The Soul

Edited by Sonya Tinsley

Illustrated by C. James Frazier

Designed by Arlene Greco

 PETER PAUPER PRESS, INC.

WHITE PLAINS, NEW YORK

First Aid
For The Soul

Introduction

Just as our bodies suffer bumps and bruises from the toil of everyday living, so do our spirits. Although we are adept at administering aspirin and bandages for our physical pain, often we are at a loss when it is our souls that are wounded. Reach for this "first aid kit" not only to nurse spiritual emergencies, but also to discourage them from arising in the first place. As the childhood rhyme reminds us, "sticks and stones may break our bones," but words can heal our hearts.

S. T.

Spiritual Refreshment

Fear less, hope more,
eat less, chew more,
whine less, breathe more,
talk less, say more, love more,
and all good things
will be yours.

SWEDISH PROVERB

One has to find a
balance between what people
need from you and what
you need for yourself.

JESSYE NORMAN

It's not the load
that breaks you down,
it's the way you carry it.

LENA HORNE

*T*o keep a lamp
burning we have to
keep putting oil in it.

MOTHER TERESA

Some women must leap,
bow, and run, for their
souls crave dance.
Yet others crave only a
tree-leaning peace.

CLARISSA PINKOLA ESTES

You must have been
warned against letting
the golden hours slip by.
Yes, but some of them
are golden only because
we let them slip.

J. M. BARRIE

If you're at the sink washing the cup, wash the cup. Don't worry about everything else. . . . We forget to appreciate the simplest moments of the day, the sublime in the ordinary.

JULIA ROBERTS

*F*inish every day and
be done with it. You have
done what you could. Some
blunders and absurdities
no doubt crept in;
forget them as soon
as you can.

RALPH WALDO EMERSON

Many persons have a
wrong idea of what constitutes
true happiness. It is not attained
through self-gratification
but through fidelity to
a worthy purpose.

HELEN KELLER

One ought every day at least,
to hear a little song,
read a good poem, see a
fine picture, and if it were
possible, to speak a few
reasonable words.

GOETHE

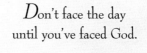

*D*on't face the day
until you've faced God.

MAYA ANGELOU

The best way to know God
is to love many things.

VINCENT VAN GOGH

When we are tired,
we are attacked by ideas
we conquered long ago.

FRIEDRICH WILHELM NIETZSCHE

The grand essentials to happiness in this life are something to do, something to love, and something to hope for.

JOSEPH ADDISON

*F*eeling rich is born of simple things: good health, comfort, freedom and laughter along with being well loved.

SARK

We all need four or five people in our lives whose faces light up when we walk into the room.

JESS LAIR

*B*e happy.
It's one way of being wise.

COLETTE

The more you praise
and celebrate your life, the
more there is in life
to celebrate.

OPRAH WINFREY

The secret of life is balance,
and the absence of balance
is life's destruction.

INAYAT KHAN

*T*he human soul has need
of security and also of risk. . . .
The boredom produced by a
complete absence of risk is
also a sickness of the soul.

SIMONE WEIL

There are only two ways to
live your life—one is as if
everything is a miracle,
the other is as though
nothing is a miracle.

ALBERT EINSTEIN

Reality is something
you rise above.

LIZA MINNELLI

It is a paradox of creative recovery that we must get serious about taking ourselves lightly. We must work at learning to play.

JULIA CAMERON

Never lose a sense of the whimsical and perilous charm of daily life, with its meetings and words and accidents.

LOGAN PEARSALL SMITH

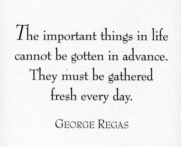

The important things in life
cannot be gotten in advance.
They must be gathered
fresh every day.

GEORGE REGAS

Self-Awareness

Great lovers realize
that they are what they
are in love with.

NATALIE GOLDBERG

Always be a first-rate version
of yourself, instead of a
second-rate version of
somebody else.

JUDY GARLAND

What a wonderful life
I've had! I only wish I'd
realized it sooner.

COLETTE

To know what you prefer
instead of humbly saying
Amen to what the world
tells you you ought to prefer,
is to have kept your soul alive.

ROBERT LOUIS STEVENSON

Develop interest in life as you see it; in people, things, literature, music—the world is so rich, simply throbbing with rich treasures, beautiful souls and interesting people. Forget yourself.

HENRY MILLER

One of the things I learned the hard way was that it doesn't pay to get discouraged. Keeping busy and making optimism a way of life can restore your faith in yourself.

LUCILLE BALL

I weep a lot.
I thank God I laugh a lot, too.
The main thing in one's
own private world is to try
to laugh as much as you cry.

MAYA ANGELOU

If you were born
without wings do nothing
to prevent their growing.

COCO CHANEL

*Y*our mind will be like its
habitual thoughts: for the soul
becomes dyed with the
color of its thoughts.

MARCUS AURELIUS

Go within every day and find
the inner strength so that
the world will not blow
your candle out.

KATHERINE DUNHAM

I'm inspired when I walk down the street and still see people trying. A lot of them look as if they're on their last leg, but they're still getting up somehow.

Faith Ringgold

We are not troubled
by things, but by the
opinions which we have
of things.

EPICTETUS

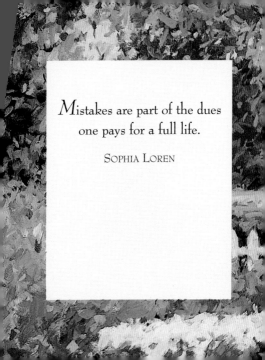

Mistakes are part of the dues
one pays for a full life.

SOPHIA LOREN

I am not a quitter.
I will fight until I drop.
It is just a matter of having
some faith in the fact that
as long as you are able to
draw breath in this universe,
you have a chance.

CICELY TYSON

Millions long for immortality who don't know what to do with themselves on a rainy Sunday afternoon.

SUSAN ERTZ

Some people change jobs,
spouses, and friends—
but never think of
changing themselves.

PAULA GIDDINGS

I like living. I have sometimes been wildly, despairingly, acutely miserable, racked with sorrow, but through it all I still know quite certainly that just to be alive is a grand thing.

AGATHA CHRISTIE

What lies behind us and what lies before us are tiny matters compared to what lies within us.

RALPH WALDO EMERSON

So many people dwell on negativity and I've survived by ignoring it . . .

JUDITH JAMISON

*I*t is better to be hated for
what you are than loved
for what you are not.

ANDRE GIDE

Cures for Crises

Noble deeds
and hot baths are
the best cures
for depression.

DODIE SMITH

Worries go down
better with soup
than without.

YIDDISH PROVERB

We learn wisdom from failure
much more than from success;
we often discover what will do
by finding out what will not do;
and probably he who never
made a mistake never
made a discovery.

SAMUEL SMILES

The world is round and
the place which may seem
like the end may also be only
the beginning.

Ivy Baker Priest

You will forget your misery;
you will remember it as waters
that have passed away.

JOB 11:16

Things fall apart so things
can fall together.

AMERICAN FOLK SAYING

When you get to wit's end,
remember that God lives there.

FOLK SAYING

Worry is interest paid on trouble before it is due.

MIRIAM MAKEBA

You will not grow if you sit in
a beautiful flower garden,
but you will grow if you are sick,
if you are in pain, if you
experience losses, and if you
do not put your head
in the sand . . .

ELIZABETH KUBLER-ROSS

What soap is for the body,
tears are for the soul.

JEWISH PROVERB

No matter how long
the winter, spring is
sure to follow.

GUINEAN PROVERB

*T*ruly, it is in the darkness that one finds the light, so when we are in sorrow, then this light is nearest of all to us.

MEISTER ECKHART

Gray skies are just
clouds passing over.

DUKE ELLINGTON

The way I see it, if you want
the rainbow, you gotta
put up with the rain.

DOLLY PARTON

*B*e glad you can suffer,
be glad you can feel. . . .
How can you tell if you're
feeling good unless you've felt
bad, so you have something
to compare it with?

THOMAS TRYON

You may think that all your happiness depends upon obtaining one particular thing in life; later on, you praise the Lord that you didn't get it.

FLORENCE SCOVEL SHINN

When the heart weeps for what it has lost, the spirit laughs for what it has found.

SUFI TEACHING

Nothing in life is to be feared.
It is only to be understood.

MARIE CURIE

It has never been, and never will be, easy work! But the road that is built in hope is more pleasant to the traveler than the road built in despair, even though they both lead to the same destination.

MARION ZIMMER BRADLEY

In three words,
I can sum up everything I've
learned about life:
It goes on.

ROBERT FROST